Mom —
1998 the year of
the great-grandchild!
Love, Sherry

ANNE GEDDES

1998
Datebook

A COLLECTION OF IMAGES

ISBN 1-55912-586-1

Please write to us for a FREE FULL COLOR CATALOG of our fine
Anne Geddes calendars and books, Cedco Publishing Company,
2955 Kerner Blvd., San Rafael, CA 94901.

The Anne Geddes 1998 A Collection of Images Datebook is owned and produced by
The Especially Kids Company Limited,
2 York Street, Parnell, Auckland, New Zealand.
Telephone 64-9-375 2566, Facsimile 64-9-375-2560

© Anne Geddes 1997

Published in 1997 by Cedco Publishing Company,
2955 Kerner Blvd, San Rafael, CA 94901.

Produced by Kel Geddes
Color separations by Image Centre
Printed in Hong Kong

is the registered trademark
of The Especially Kids Company Limited

ANNE GEDDES

Anne has been very successful in forming a special relationship with the American public. Appearances on a host of television and radio stations and articles in a range of newspapers and magazines attest to the reputation that this extraordinary Australian-born photographer has achieved with her images.

This collection of special images demonstrates clearly the rapport Anne has with children. This rapport, coupled with Anne's excellent photographic skills have led to her critical acclaim as the preeminent photographer in the world today.

1998

JANUARY

S	M	T	W	T	F	S
				1	2	3
4	5	6	7	8	9	10
11	12	13	14	15	16	17
18	19	20	21	22	23	24
25	26	27	28	29	30	31

FEBRUARY

S	M	T	W	T	F	S
1	2	3	4	5	6	7
8	9	10	11	12	13	14
15	16	17	18	19	20	21
22	23	24	25	26	27	28

MARCH

S	M	T	W	T	F	S
1	2	3	4	5	6	7
8	9	10	11	12	13	14
15	16	17	18	19	20	21
22	23	24	25	26	27	28
29	30	31				

APRIL

S	M	T	W	T	F	S
			1	2	3	4
5	6	7	8	9	10	11
12	13	14	15	16	17	18
19	20	21	22	23	24	25
26	27	28	29	30		

MAY

S	M	T	W	T	F	S
31					1	2
3	4	5	6	7	8	9
10	11	12	13	14	15	16
17	18	19	20	21	22	23
24	25	26	27	28	29	30

JUNE

S	M	T	W	T	F	S
	1	2	3	4	5	6
7	8	9	10	11	12	13
14	15	16	17	18	19	20
21	22	23	24	25	26	27
28	29	30				

JULY

S	M	T	W	T	F	S
			1	2	3	4
5	6	7	8	9	10	11
12	13	14	15	16	17	18
19	20	21	22	23	24	25
26	27	28	29	30	31	

AUGUST

S	M	T	W	T	F	S
30	31					1
2	3	4	5	6	7	8
9	10	11	12	13	14	15
16	17	18	19	20	21	22
23	24	25	26	27	28	29

SEPTEMBER

S	M	T	W	T	F	S
		1	2	3	4	5
6	7	8	9	10	11	12
13	14	15	16	17	18	19
20	21	22	23	24	25	26
27	28	29	30			

OCTOBER

S	M	T	W	T	F	S
				1	2	3
4	5	6	7	8	9	10
11	12	13	14	15	16	17
18	19	20	21	22	23	24
25	26	27	28	29	30	31

NOVEMBER

S	M	T	W	T	F	S
1	2	3	4	5	6	7
8	9	10	11	12	13	14
15	16	17	18	19	20	21
22	23	24	25	26	27	28
29	30					

DECEMBER

S	M	T	W	T	F	S
		1	2	3	4	5
6	7	8	9	10	11	12
13	14	15	16	17	18	19
20	21	22	23	24	25	26
27	28	29	30	31		

December

SUNDAY 21 Have received many cards and
Winter Solstice
3:09 PM E.S.T. wishes from dear friends. Have done
a minimum amount of Christmas decorating as
we plan to be away for Christmas. Lights and
Last Quarter bows on carriage lamp.

MONDAY 22 Have exchanged gifts with Helen
and she brought her lovely wreath for
my front porch. She has made these
wreathes for years and years — I usually
keep mine around long past the holidays

TUESDAY 23 Lunch at loft — Helen, Sherry and I.
Hanukkah
(begins at sunset) Margaret already on her way to valley to be
with family. Autumn and Jessie here — invited to lunch
but they went ice skating at Pound Valley. Autumn
gave me lovely green robe — velour.

WEDNESDAY 24 Here we are in Reno Peppermill
Hotel on 5th floor. Lovely view — some snow earlier
— now clear in eve. Bob's b.d. so he chose buffett
at Eldorado. Good food — lots of choices. Had some
time at Thrift stores today.

THURSDAY 25 Lite breakfast in our hotel. Saw 2 movies at
nearby theaters. 'Titanic' — 3 hrs. 'As good as it gets' — 2½ hrs.
Christmas Day no shopping today. Enjoyed relaxing — view. Presents
this book from S&B. They got 'Trivial Pursuit' from A + F. I gave
them this 2 night stay here in Peppermill. Dinner here
at Buffet. Simply delightful — duck and too much dessert.

FRIDAY 26 Shopping day. Fun in 'Play it again kids'.
Boxing Day (Canada) I bought a ski jacket. Replaced a fry pan.
X.mas sale at Ben Franklin. — food at Trader Joes.
I'd never been to this store. Gourmet food. Dinner at
Atlantis buffet. More taste treats. Outside we either has
been about 19° Cold. — but sunny. Home at 7 pm.

SATURDAY 27 Home again. Autumn
leaving Sun. morn. They had
a lovely day skiing and much
ice skating while here.

JANUARY						
S	M	T	W	T	F	S
				1	2	3
4	5	6	7	8	9	10
11	12	13	14	15	16	17
18	19	20	21	22	23	24
25	26	27	28	29	30	31

December - January

SUNDAY 28 *Routine —*

MONDAY 29 *Things back in order after trip.*

● New Moon

TUESDAY 30 *Lunch w/H. M. & Sh. — exchanging Christmas Stories.*

WEDNESDAY 31 *New Years eve. — watching T.V. until 12:00*

THURSDAY 1 *Hello 98! Looking for good year. 97*
New Year's Day *was marred by devastating floods beginning on Jan 1st. I am remembering that Jack left at 8 A.M. this day 6 yrs. ago. Every day I see evidence of good things he did around here. I hope I made him realize how much I appreciated them.*

FRIDAY 2 *Raining — not flooding*
Sat 3 belongs here —

SATURDAY 3 *Lovely elegant dinner at S&B. Shrimp & Scallops out of my freezer. Sh. made noodles and pecan pumpkin pie — most delicious w/David & Sandy   Rain*

		JANUARY				
S	M	T	W	T	F	S
				1	2	3
4	5	6	7	8	9	10
11	12	13	14	15	16	17
18	19	20	21	22	23	24
25	26	27	28	29	30	31

January

SUNDAY 4 *Lazy day — awoke to 5 in snow,*
Very beautiful — fire in fireplace
not so lazy after all — worked with wood
snowed most of day — not much more accumulation tho

MONDAY 5

◐
First Quarter

TUESDAY 6
Snow

WEDNESDAY 7
Rain

THURSDAY 8
Rain

FRIDAY 9
Rain + Snow

SATURDAY 10 *Talked to Selma. She has a*
mild sore throat — talked mostly about
Sonny Bono funeral

SUNDAY 11

More rain + fog - noon

MONDAY 12

Raining quite hard - morning
Put in order to sell 200 sha NSP if it goes to 26½

○
Full Moon

TUESDAY 13

Lunch (4)

Rain

Sherry having trouble - heart flutters

WEDNESDAY 14

Rain
Sherry saw a clear sky after dark this night

THURSDAY 15

Rain
Bought Boeing stock @ 45⅞
Sold NSP @ 26¼

FRIDAY 16

David put louvers in pocket door to be ready
for installing new gas water heater. Free
(The water heater is promotional deal w/ Coast Gas.

SATURDAY 17

			JANUARY			
S	M	T	W	T	F	S
				1	2	3
4	5	6	7	8	9	10
11	12	13	14	15	16	17
18	19	20	21	22	23	24
25	26	27	28	29	30	31

January

SUNDAY 18

Rain

MONDAY 19

Light snow last night

TUESDAY 20

◐
Last Quarter

WEDNESDAY 21

Sherry appt. w/ Zimmet
weather OK — and roads

THURSDAY 22

Sh needs to have appt w/ Cardiologist

FRIDAY 23

New gas water heater today! Free from East Gas.
Promotion deal   S + D left for 3 days in SF.
No Rain or Snow.   good fun

SATURDAY 24

Rain hard last nite
2 + 3 A.M.

		JANUARY				
S	M	T	W	T	F	S
				1	2	3
4	5	6	7	8	9	10
11	12	13	14	15	16	17
18	19	20	21	22	23	24
25	26	27	28	29	30	31

January

SUNDAY 25

MONDAY 26

TUESDAY 27

Lunch for 3. Sherry not feeling well

WEDNESDAY 28

S + B leave for Reno — stay 2 nites at Silverado
for appt w/ Cardiologist & Ear, Nose & throat for Bob.

● New Moon

THURSDAY 29

Sherry appt. w/ Heart Dr
Bob appt w/ ear, nose & Throat Dr.

FRIDAY 30

9AM Wet Snow
3PM — a bit of Sun

SATURDAY 31

		JANUARY				
S	M	T	W	T	F	S
				1	2	3
4	5	6	7	8	9	10
11	12	13	14	15	16	17
18	19	20	21	22	23	24
25	26	27	28	29	30	31

February

SUNDAY 1 Rain

MONDAY 2 Sun

TUESDAY 3 Rain - not hard

◑
First Quarter

WEDNESDAY 4

Sun. went shopping.
Surprise! Sherry has word that labor started at 4:30
p.m. Florence in hosp. by 6. 10 days before Dr. date.

THURSDAY 5 Snow - lite. Baby Malo David Roger born
3:15 A.M. All well! 11 hrs. after labor began. We have wt. in
kilos - haven't got it in lbs. yet.
Busy sending out the word. They stay in hosp min. of 5 days.

FRIDAY 6 Kelly called - much appreciated! all going well.
'They' to come home Tues. Good baby - no fuss. Nursing well.
Length is 53½ centimeters   Wt 3.888 kilo - 8.55 lb.
— inches

SATURDAY 7

SUNDAY 8

*Rod called. Jeff all set in good work.
Contractor — manager for building
projects within a Company. Tommy is to
work in Same. Moved into a house. Kids like the
school*

MONDAY 9

Nice day — Sun

TUESDAY 10

Morning — Snow

WEDNESDAY 11

○
Full Moon

THURSDAY 12

Lincoln's Birthday

FRIDAY 13

SATURDAY 14

St. Valentine's Day

FEBRUARY						
S	M	T	W	T	F	S
1	2	3	4	5	6	7
8	9	10	11	12	13	14
15	16	17	18	19	20	21
22	23	24	25	26	27	28

February

SUNDAY 15

MONDAY 16

Presidents' Day

TUESDAY 17

WEDNESDAY 18

THURSDAY 19

◑
Last Quarter

FRIDAY 20

SATURDAY 21

FEBRUARY						
S	M	T	W	T	F	S
1	2	3	4	5	6	7
8	9	10	11	12	13	14
15	16	17	18	19	20	21
22	23	24	25	26	27	28

February

SUNDAY 22
Washington's Birthday
Called Malo in France. They are all doing well. A walk outside today. Malo nursing often. Probably natural. Meant to suggest ways of stimulating the baby - ie - exercising legs and arms - talking to and singing - happy faces. They are already doing all of that.

MONDAY 23
Snow! 4 or 5 in.

TUESDAY 24
To Rene of or lunch and movie w/ Bob and Sh. Roads not bad

WEDNESDAY 25
Ash Wednesday
More light snow.

THURSDAY 26
Sherry bought our ticket to France today - leaves 3-23 for 1c days - France

● *New Moon*

FRIDAY 27

SATURDAY 28
Snow - 4"

FEBRUARY						
S	M	T	W	T	F	S
1	2	3	4	5	6	7
8	9	10	11	12	13	14
15	16	17	18	19	20	21
22	23	24	25	26	27	28

March

SUNDAY 1

Kelly gets set up with E mail at home

MONDAY 2

TUESDAY 3

Windy

WEDNESDAY 4

windy.

THURSDAY 5

Snow 6"
Looks like a fairy land this AM

◗ First Quarter

FRIDAY 6

Sun

SATURDAY 7

Talked to Velma — good —

			MARCH			
S	M	T	W	T	F	S
1	2	3	4	5	6	7
8	9	10	11	12	13	14
15	16	17	18	19	20	21
22	23	24	25	26	27	28
29	30	31				

Mostly bad weather. Rain - Fog and sometimes Sun

SUNDAY 8

MONDAY 9

TUESDAY 10

WEDNESDAY 11

THURSDAY 12

○
Full Moon

FRIDAY 13

SATURDAY 14

March

SUNDAY 15

MONDAY 16

TUESDAY 17

St. Patrick's Day

WEDNESDAY 18

THURSDAY 19

FRIDAY 20

Vernal Equinox 2:56 p.m. E.S.T.

SATURDAY 21

Last Quarter

SUNDAY 22

MONDAY 23 *S. & B to Reno –*

TUESDAY 24 *Sh plane leaves at 11 instead of 10 AM. Bad weather in S.F. No one met her in S.F. As planned. Made it to other termus.*

WEDNESDAY 25

THURSDAY 26

FRIDAY 27 *4 in. Snow! melts fast next day –*

●
New Moon

SATURDAY 28 *been out all day*

March - April

SUNDAY 29 Lovely day. Cold. breeze. Long walk.

MONDAY 30 Bob to dinner. Decent day. Green house heating.

TUESDAY 31 Rain + fog — can't see Hough. Washer + dryer to be delivered today but not if raining. Tried to call Cavillion for 40 min. never got thru. one added number to their number. Operator — never figured out why call not going thru. Sh. Starts home Thursday.

WEDNESDAY 1 Washer + dryer delivered yesterday 6 P.M. Dry to be fixed with gas today.
Heard from Sherry — Cavillion France. All going well there. Starts for Paris today. Plane leaves for home Thurs.

THURSDAY 2 Sherry back to Reno. Plane 2 hrs. late in S.F.
S + B stay over in Reno
On way over she was up for 33 hrs!

FRIDAY 3 Sherry home! Looks fine. Good in Cavillion Luggage not lost (it was in Paris and delivered next day.

◑ First Quarter

SATURDAY 4

		APRIL				
S	M	T	W	T	F	S
			1	2	3	4
5	6	7	8	9	10	11
12	13	14	15	16	17	18
19	20	21	22	23	24	25
26	27	28	29	30		

April

SUNDAY 5   *Malo 2 mo. today. 15 lbs - 24" long*

MONDAY 6   *rainy*

TUESDAY 7   *Sun - windy*

WEDNESDAY 8   *Bob - appendectomy today. Went well taking anti-biotic.*

THURSDAY 9   *Bob doing OK -*

FRIDAY 10   *Bob - temp - again came home*

SATURDAY 11   *Trouble w/ a-biotic. Dr. taking him off of it*

SUNDAY 12 *Snow lightly —*
Easter
Bob has thrush — diarrea.

MONDAY 13

Easter Monday (Canada)

TUESDAY 14

WEDNESDAY 15 *Bob back in hosp. Infection. Taking*
2 anti-biotics in vein.

THURSDAY 16

FRIDAY 17 *Bob home — Taking no anti-biotics.*
No appetite — no taste.

SATURDAY 18
So-So

			APRIL			
S	M	T	W	T	F	S
			1	2	3	4
5	6	7	8	9	10	11
12	13	14	15	16	17	18
19	20	21	22	23	24	25
26	27	28	29	30		

April

SUNDAY 19

Bob getting better —

◑
Last Quarter

MONDAY 20

Continue

TUESDAY 21

WEDNESDAY 22

Earth Day

THURSDAY 23

FRIDAY 24

National Arbor Day

SATURDAY 25

Bob OK.

			APRIL			
S	M	T	W	T	F	S
			1	2	3	4
5	6	7	8	9	10	11
12	13	14	15	16	17	18
19	20	21	22	23	24	25
26	27	28	29	30		

April - May

SUNDAY 26

New Moon

MONDAY 27

TUESDAY 28

WEDNESDAY 29

THURSDAY 30

FRIDAY 1 Sherry goes to hosp. in ambulance
with another heart episode. (3 paramedics)
Dr. got her stabalized so did not have to stay
in hosp. overnight

SATURDAY 2
Needs to make appt. with
Electrophysist in Reno.

			MAY			
S	M	T	W	T	F	S
31					1	2
3	4	5	6	7	8	9
10	11	12	13	14	15	16
17	18	19	20	21	22	23
24	25	26	27	28	29	30

May

SUNDAY 3
Not feeling well from the Tenormin. they gave her this time

First Quarter

MONDAY 4
Not feeling good. Got Appt. to see Dr. 11 A.M. Tues.

TUESDAY 5
Still not feeling well. Dr examines — sets her up for procedure 11 AM next Tues. Said not to take Tenormin any more. yay! Took camper to Reno.

WEDNESDAY 6
Not too well but some better. Needs to get Tenormin out of system. Stay over in Reno. Sees 2 movies — checks out Boom Town.

THURSDAY 7
Home late aft.
Feeling so - so —

Had hardest rain and hail shower I've ever seen yesterday. Didn't last over 15 min but - much rain & hail.

FRIDAY 8
Some better -

SATURDAY 9
Pretty good

SUNDAY 10 *Rod Starts trip to Topaz*

Mother's Day

MONDAY 11

○
Full Moon

TUESDAY 12 *Sherry appt — Dr. did procedure.*
Closed elec pathways he thot would remedy the problem.
Uh-oh. More atrial fibs after his operation

WEDNESDAY 13 *Sh. still fibrilating. Dr.*
goes back in and closes more
pathways — also installed pace-
maker at same time.

THURSDAY 14
Still fibs — but Dr. thinks she will
be OK as body adjusts. No more
Lenoxin (Good)

FRIDAY 15 *Released — comes home. Feels better —*
Not par yet

SATURDAY 16 *We all met R & N in Reno*
for lunch at Nugget. Then to Redin
exhibit. Saw Horse Whisperers at New
theatre after R & N. leave. Good
Raging snow storm on way home
David couldn't see road. Got home 11 pm.

MAY						
S	M	T	W	T	F	S
31					1	2
3	4	5	6	7	8	9
10	11	12	13	14	15	16
17	18	19	20	21	22	23
24	25	26	27	28	29	30

May

SUNDAY 17 Sh. better ea. day.

MONDAY 18
Victoria Day (Canada) weather better

TUESDAY 19

◑
Last Quarter

WEDNESDAY 20 Sh. appt to see pace-maker technician. It.
had recorded some fibs but she said leads were
sealing fine — no gardening for next 6 wks! Sh. sez
may as well go camping — Brought home new Cat — got it

THURSDAY 21

FRIDAY 22 S & B leave for Reno again to get cat
spayed and then take off camping.
Lite rain here Fri. nite

SATURDAY 23
OK. Cloudy

		MAY				
S	M	T	W	T	F	S
31					1	2
3	4	5	6	7	8	9
10	11	12	13	14	15	16
17	18	19	20	21	22	23
24	25	26	27	28	29	30

May

SUNDAY 24 *Rain - lt. afternoon. One in. this nite.*

MONDAY 25 *Cloudy - lt. rain. Rain again nite.*
Memorial Day *S + B drive to Bucks, 2 ft. of snow there.*

●
New Moon

TUESDAY 26 *Early morn, - rain - Snowing at noon.*
Walked to Morn. Thunder for lunch in big snow
flakes - back home in rain & snow. More rain.
More rain - snow late eve.

WEDNESDAY 27 *Lt. rain morning*

THURSDAY 28

FRIDAY 29

SATURDAY 30

			MAY			
S	M	T	W	T	F	S
31					1	2
3	4	5	6	7	8	9
10	11	12	13	14	15	16
17	18	19	20	21	22	23
24	25	26	27	28	29	30

May - June

SUNDAY 31

Pentecost

MONDAY 1

◑
First Quarter

TUESDAY 2

WEDNESDAY 3

THURSDAY 4

FRIDAY 5

SATURDAY 6

SUNDAY 7

MONDAY 8

TUESDAY 9 *S & B return from camping.*
Thinks pace maker will need adjusting

WEDNESDAY 10
Rainy day — dreary

○
Full Moon

THURSDAY 11

FRIDAY 12

SATURDAY 13

JUNE						
S	M	T	W	T	F	S
	1	2	3	4	5	6
7	8	9	10	11	12	13
14	15	16	17	18	19	20
21	22	23	24	25	26	27
28	29	30				

June

Flag Day

MONDAY 15

TUESDAY 16

WEDNESDAY 17

◖
Last Quarter

THURSDAY 18

FRIDAY 19

SATURDAY 20

SUNDAY 21

Summer Solstice 10:04 a.m. E.D.T
Father's Day

MONDAY 22

TUESDAY 23

●

New Moon

WEDNESDAY 24

St. Jean Baptiste Day (Quebec)

THURSDAY 25

FRIDAY 26

SATURDAY 27

			JUNE			
S	M	T	W	T	F	S
	1	2	3	4	5	6
7	8	9	10	11	12	13
14	15	16	17	18	19	20
21	22	23	24	25	26	27
28	29	30				

June - July

SUNDAY 28

MONDAY 29

TUESDAY 30

WEDNESDAY 1

Canada Day (Canada)

First Quarter

THURSDAY 2

FRIDAY 3

SATURDAY 4

Independence Day

			JULY			
S	M	T	W	T	F	S
			1	2	3	4
5	6	7	8	9	10	11
12	13	14	15	16	17	18
19	20	21	22	23	24	25
26	27	28	29	30	31	

July

SUNDAY 5

MONDAY 6

TUESDAY 7

WEDNESDAY 8

THURSDAY 9

○
Full Moon

FRIDAY 10

SATURDAY 11

SUNDAY 12

MONDAY 13

TUESDAY 14

WEDNESDAY 15

THURSDAY 16

Last Quarter

FRIDAY 17

SATURDAY 18

JULY						
S	M	T	W	T	F	S
			1	2	3	4
5	6	7	8	9	10	11
12	13	14	15	16	17	18
19	20	21	22	23	24	25
26	27	28	29	30	31	

July

SUNDAY 19

MONDAY 20

TUESDAY 21

WEDNESDAY 22

THURSDAY 23

New Moon

FRIDAY 24

SATURDAY 25

JULY						
S	M	T	W	T	F	S
			1	2	3	4
5	6	7	8	9	10	11
12	13	14	15	16	17	18
19	20	21	22	23	24	25
26	27	28	29	30	31	

July - August

SUNDAY 26

MONDAY 27

TUESDAY 28

WEDNESDAY 29

THURSDAY 30

FRIDAY 31

◐
First Quarter

SATURDAY 1

AUGUST						
S	M	T	W	T	F	S
30	31					1
2	3	4	5	6	7	8
9	10	11	12	13	14	15
16	17	18	19	20	21	22
23	24	25	26	27	28	29

August

SUNDAY 2

MONDAY 3

TUESDAY 4

WEDNESDAY 5

THURSDAY 6

FRIDAY 7

○
Full Moon

SATURDAY 8

SUNDAY 9

MONDAY 10

TUESDAY 11

WEDNESDAY 12

THURSDAY 13

FRIDAY 14

◐
Last Quarter

SATURDAY 15

			AUGUST			
S	M	T	W	T	F	S
30	31					1
2	3	4	5	6	7	8
9	10	11	12	13	14	15
16	17	18	19	20	21	22
23	24	25	26	27	28	29

August

SUNDAY 16

MONDAY 17

TUESDAY 18

WEDNESDAY 19

THURSDAY 20

FRIDAY 21

New Moon

SATURDAY 22

SUNDAY 23

MONDAY 24

TUESDAY 25

WEDNESDAY 26

THURSDAY 27

FRIDAY 28

SATURDAY 29

AUGUST						
S	M	T	W	T	F	S
30	31					1
2	3	4	5	6	7	8
9	10	11	12	13	14	15
16	17	18	19	20	21	22
23	24	25	26	27	28	29

August - September

SUNDAY 30

◑
First Quarter

MONDAY 31

TUESDAY 1

WEDNESDAY 2

THURSDAY 3

FRIDAY 4

SATURDAY 5

SEPTEMBER						
S	M	T	W	T	F	S
		1	2	3	4	5
6	7	8	9	10	11	12
13	14	15	16	17	18	19
20	21	22	23	24	25	26
27	28	29	30			

September

SUNDAY 6

○
Full Moon

MONDAY 7

Labor Day

TUESDAY 8

WEDNESDAY 9

THURSDAY 10

FRIDAY 11

SATURDAY 12

◖
Last Quarter

		SEPTEMBER				
S	M	T	W	T	F	S
		1	2	3	4	5
6	7	8	9	10	11	12
13	14	15	16	17	18	19
20	21	22	23	24	25	26
27	28	29	30			

September

SUNDAY 13

Grandparents' Day

MONDAY 14

TUESDAY 15

WEDNESDAY 16

THURSDAY 17

FRIDAY 18

SATURDAY 19

SUNDAY 20

Rosh Hashanah (begins at sunset)

●

New Moon

MONDAY 21

TUESDAY 22

WEDNESDAY 23

Autumnal Equinox 1:39 a.m. E.D.T.

THURSDAY 24

FRIDAY 25

SATURDAY 26

SEPTEMBER						
S	M	T	W	T	F	S
		1	2	3	4	5
6	7	8	9	10	11	12
13	14	15	16	17	18	19
20	21	22	23	24	25	26
27	28	29	30			

September - October

SUNDAY 27

MONDAY 28

◑
First Quarter

TUESDAY 29

Yom Kippur (begins at sunset)

WEDNESDAY 30

THURSDAY 1

FRIDAY 2

SATURDAY 3

OCTOBER						
S	M	T	W	T	F	S
				1	2	3
4	5	6	7	8	9	10
11	12	13	14	15	16	17
18	19	20	21	22	23	24
25	26	27	28	29	30	31

October

SUNDAY 4

MONDAY 5

○
Full Moon

TUESDAY 6

WEDNESDAY 7

THURSDAY 8

FRIDAY 9

SATURDAY 10

OCTOBER						
S	M	T	W	T	F	S
				1	2	3
4	5	6	7	8	9	10
11	12	13	14	15	16	17
18	19	20	21	22	23	24
25	26	27	28	29	30	31

SUNDAY 11

MONDAY 12

Columbus Day
Canadian Thanksgiving Day

Last Quarter

TUESDAY 13

WEDNESDAY 14

THURSDAY 15

FRIDAY 16

SATURDAY 17

October

SUNDAY 18

MONDAY 19

TUESDAY 20

●
New Moon

WEDNESDAY 21

THURSDAY 22

FRIDAY 23

SATURDAY 24

			OCTOBER			
S	M	T	W	T	F	S
				1	2	3
4	5	6	7	8	9	10
11	12	13	14	15	16	17
18	19	20	21	22	23	24
25	26	27	28	29	30	31

October

SUNDAY 25

Daylight Saving Time ends in U.S.A. (subtract 1 hour from clock)

MONDAY 26

TUESDAY 27

WEDNESDAY 28

First Quarter

THURSDAY 29

FRIDAY 30

SATURDAY 31

Halloween

			OCTOBER			
S	M	T	W	T	F	S
				1	2	3
4	5	6	7	8	9	10
11	12	13	14	15	16	17
18	19	20	21	22	23	24
25	26	27	28	29	30	31

November

SUNDAY 1

MONDAY 2

TUESDAY 3

Election Day

WEDNESDAY 4

○
Full Moon

THURSDAY 5

FRIDAY 6

SATURDAY 7

SUNDAY 8

MONDAY 9

TUESDAY 10

◑
Last Quarter

WEDNESDAY 11

Veterans Day
Remembrance Day (Canada)

THURSDAY 12

FRIDAY 13

SATURDAY 14

NOVEMBER						
S	M	T	W	T	F	S
1	2	3	4	5	6	7
8	9	10	11	12	13	14
15	16	17	18	19	20	21
22	23	24	25	26	27	28
29	30					

November

SUNDAY 15

MONDAY 16

TUESDAY 17

WEDNESDAY 18

●
New Moon

THURSDAY 19

FRIDAY 20

SATURDAY 21

SUNDAY 22

MONDAY 23

TUESDAY 24

WEDNESDAY 25

THURSDAY 26

Thanksgiving Day

◐

First Quarter

FRIDAY 27

SATURDAY 28

NOVEMBER						
S	M	T	W	T	F	S
1	2	3	4	5	6	7
8	9	10	11	12	13	14
15	16	17	18	19	20	21
22	23	24	25	26	27	28
29	30					

November - December

SUNDAY 29

MONDAY 30

TUESDAY 1

WEDNESDAY 2

THURSDAY 3

○
Full Moon

FRIDAY 4

SATURDAY 5

DECEMBER						
S	M	T	W	T	F	S
		1	2	3	4	5
6	7	8	9	10	11	12
13	14	15	16	17	18	19
20	21	22	23	24	25	26
27	28	29	30	31		

December

SUNDAY 6

MONDAY 7

TUESDAY 8

WEDNESDAY 9

THURSDAY 10

◑
Last Quarter

FRIDAY 11

SATURDAY 12

DECEMBER						
S	M	T	W	T	F	S
		1	2	3	4	5
6	7	8	9	10	11	12
13	14	15	16	17	18	19
20	21	22	23	24	25	26
27	28	29	30	31		

SUNDAY 13

Hanukkah (begins at sunset)

MONDAY 14

TUESDAY 15

WEDNESDAY 16

THURSDAY 17

FRIDAY 18

New Moon

SATURDAY 19

December

SUNDAY 20

MONDAY 21

Winter Solstice 8:58 p.m. E.S.T.

TUESDAY 22

WEDNESDAY 23

THURSDAY 24

FRIDAY 25

Christmas Day

SATURDAY 26

Boxing Day (Canada)

◐

First Quarter

			DECEMBER			
S	M	T	W	T	F	S
		1	2	3	4	5
6	7	8	9	10	11	12
13	14	15	16	17	18	19
20	21	22	23	24	25	26
27	28	29	30	31		

December - January

SUNDAY 27

MONDAY 28

TUESDAY 29

WEDNESDAY 30

THURSDAY 31

FRIDAY 1

New Year's Day

SATURDAY 2

JANUARY						
S	M	T	W	T	F	S
31					1	2
3	4	5	6	7	8	9
10	11	12	13	14	15	16
17	18	19	20	21	22	23
24	25	26	27	28	29	30

1999

JANUARY
S	M	T	W	T	F	S
31					1	2
3	4	5	6	7	8	9
10	11	12	13	14	15	16
17	18	19	20	21	22	23
24	25	26	27	28	29	30

FEBRUARY
S	M	T	W	T	F	S
	1	2	3	4	5	6
7	8	9	10	11	12	13
14	15	16	17	18	19	20
21	22	23	24	25	26	27
28						

MARCH
S	M	T	W	T	F	S
	1	2	3	4	5	6
7	8	9	10	11	12	13
14	15	16	17	18	19	20
21	22	23	24	25	26	27
28	29	30	31			

APRIL
S	M	T	W	T	F	S
				1	2	3
4	5	6	7	8	9	10
11	12	13	14	15	16	17
18	19	20	21	22	23	24
25	26	27	28	29	30	

MAY
S	M	T	W	T	F	S
30	31					1
2	3	4	5	6	7	8
9	10	11	12	13	14	15
16	17	18	19	20	21	22
23	24	25	26	27	28	29

JUNE
S	M	T	W	T	F	S
		1	2	3	4	5
6	7	8	9	10	11	12
13	14	15	16	17	18	19
20	21	22	23	24	25	26
27	28	29	30			

JULY
S	M	T	W	T	F	S
				1	2	3
4	5	6	7	8	9	10
11	12	13	14	15	16	17
18	19	20	21	22	23	24
25	26	27	28	29	30	31

AUGUST
S	M	T	W	T	F	S
1	2	3	4	5	6	7
8	9	10	11	12	13	14
15	16	17	18	19	20	21
22	23	24	25	26	27	28
29	30	31				

SEPTEMBER
S	M	T	W	T	F	S
			1	2	3	4
5	6	7	8	9	10	11
12	13	14	15	16	17	18
19	20	21	22	23	24	25
26	27	28	29	30		

OCTOBER
S	M	T	W	T	F	S
31					1	2
3	4	5	6	7	8	9
10	11	12	13	14	15	16
17	18	19	20	21	22	23
24	25	26	27	28	29	30

NOVEMBER
S	M	T	W	T	F	S
	1	2	3	4	5	6
7	8	9	10	11	12	13
14	15	16	17	18	19	20
21	22	23	24	25	26	27
28	29	30				

DECEMBER
S	M	T	W	T	F	S
			1	2	3	4
5	6	7	8	9	10	11
12	13	14	15	16	17	18
19	20	21	22	23	24	25
26	27	28	29	30	31	

2000

JANUARY
S	M	T	W	T	F	S
30	31					1
2	3	4	5	6	7	8
9	10	11	12	13	14	15
16	17	18	19	20	21	22
23	24	25	26	27	28	29

FEBRUARY
S	M	T	W	T	F	S
		1	2	3	4	5
6	7	8	9	10	11	12
13	14	15	16	17	18	19
20	21	22	23	24	25	26
27	28	29				

MARCH
S	M	T	W	T	F	S
			1	2	3	4
5	6	7	8	9	10	11
12	13	14	15	16	17	18
19	20	21	22	23	24	25
26	27	28	29	30	31	

APRIL
S	M	T	W	T	F	S
30						1
2	3	4	5	6	7	8
9	10	11	12	13	14	15
16	17	18	19	20	21	22
23	24	25	26	27	28	29

MAY
S	M	T	W	T	F	S
	1	2	3	4	5	6
7	8	9	10	11	12	13
14	15	16	17	18	19	20
21	22	23	24	25	26	27
28	29	30	31			

JUNE
S	M	T	W	T	F	S
				1	2	3
4	5	6	7	8	9	10
11	12	13	14	15	16	17
18	19	20	21	22	23	24
25	26	27	28	29	30	

JULY
S	M	T	W	T	F	S
30	31					1
2	3	4	5	6	7	8
9	10	11	12	13	14	15
16	17	18	19	20	21	22
23	24	25	26	27	28	29

AUGUST
S	M	T	W	T	F	S
		1	2	3	4	5
6	7	8	9	10	11	12
13	14	15	16	17	18	19
20	21	22	23	24	25	26
27	28	29	30	31		

SEPTEMBER
S	M	T	W	T	F	S
					1	2
3	4	5	6	7	8	9
10	11	12	13	14	15	16
17	18	19	20	21	22	23
24	25	26	27	28	29	30

OCTOBER
S	M	T	W	T	F	S
1	2	3	4	5	6	7
8	9	10	11	12	13	14
15	16	17	18	19	20	21
22	23	24	25	26	27	28
29	30	31				

NOVEMBER
S	M	T	W	T	F	S
			1	2	3	4
5	6	7	8	9	10	11
12	13	14	15	16	17	18
19	20	21	22	23	24	25
26	27	28	29	30		

DECEMBER
S	M	T	W	T	F	S
31					1	2
3	4	5	6	7	8	9
10	11	12	13	14	15	16
17	18	19	20	21	22	23
24	25	26	27	28	29	30

2001

JANUARY
S	M	T	W	T	F	S
	1	2	3	4	5	6
7	8	9	10	11	12	13
14	15	16	17	18	19	20
21	22	23	24	25	26	27
28	29	30	31			

FEBRUARY
S	M	T	W	T	F	S
				1	2	3
4	5	6	7	8	9	10
11	12	13	14	15	16	17
18	19	20	21	22	23	24
25	26	27	28			

MARCH
S	M	T	W	T	F	S
				1	2	3
4	5	6	7	8	9	10
11	12	13	14	15	16	17
18	19	20	21	22	23	24
25	26	27	28	29	30	31

APRIL
S	M	T	W	T	F	S
1	2	3	4	5	6	7
8	9	10	11	12	13	14
15	16	17	18	19	20	21
22	23	24	25	26	27	28
29	30					

MAY
S	M	T	W	T	F	S
		1	2	3	4	5
6	7	8	9	10	11	12
13	14	15	16	17	18	19
20	21	22	23	24	25	26
27	28	29	30	31		

JUNE
S	M	T	W	T	F	S
					1	2
3	4	5	6	7	8	9
10	11	12	13	14	15	16
17	18	19	20	21	22	23
24	25	26	27	28	29	30

JULY
S	M	T	W	T	F	S
1	2	3	4	5	6	7
8	9	10	11	12	13	14
15	16	17	18	19	20	21
22	23	24	25	26	27	28
29	30	31				

AUGUST
S	M	T	W	T	F	S
			1	2	3	4
5	6	7	8	9	10	11
12	13	14	15	16	17	18
19	20	21	22	23	24	25
26	27	28	29	30	31	

SEPTEMBER
S	M	T	W	T	F	S
30						1
2	3	4	5	6	7	8
9	10	11	12	13	14	15
16	17	18	19	20	21	22
23	24	25	26	27	28	29

OCTOBER
S	M	T	W	T	F	S
	1	2	3	4	5	6
7	8	9	10	11	12	13
14	15	16	17	18	19	20
21	22	23	24	25	26	27
28	29	30	31			

NOVEMBER
S	M	T	W	T	F	S
				1	2	3
4	5	6	7	8	9	10
11	12	13	14	15	16	17
18	19	20	21	22	23	24
25	26	27	28	29	30	

DECEMBER
S	M	T	W	T	F	S
30	31					1
2	3	4	5	6	7	8
9	10	11	12	13	14	15
16	17	18	19	20	21	22
23	24	25	26	27	28	29